UNBELIEVABLE FACTS ABOUT PAST AND PRESENT U.S PRESIDENTS FOR KIDS

Amazing, Interesting, and Fun History Trivia You Need to Know About American Leaders with Quiz Questions.

Kids Intelligentsia

Alpha Zuriel Publishing

TABLE OF CONTENTS

INTRODUCTION

The United States has seen some great men ruled her over the centuries, from George Washington to Joe Biden. We will look briefly into each of the past 45 U.S presidents' history and myths and facts, as well as the present president.

GEORGE WASHINGTON

From 1789 to 1797

Virginia,

Independent

The 'father of the country' for the United States of America is the great George Washington.

Despite losing his parents when he was a teenager, Washington was a rich, powerful man and the owner of large numbers of slaves who did not know freedom until several decades later.

Fact: He wrote the Constitution of the United States that has been in effect for more than 200 years.

He also had poor, decaying teeth, so he wore dentures made from spring, ivory, and brass screws.

JOHN ADAMS

From 1797 to 1801

Massachusetts

Federalist

After being the vice president of Washington, John Adams was the second man to take

the United States of America's reins. However, in his political career, an abrupt episode marked a turning point in destiny: The Boston Massacre. This earned him a strong loss of prestige over the years.

Fact: He began his political career in the War of Independence and was the American union's first vice president.

His last words were, "Thomas Jefferson survives." But he didn't know that Jefferson Thomas had died a few hours before.

THOMAS JEFFERSON

1801-1809

Virginia

Democrat-Republican

This prolific and revolutionary Republican came to power after John Adams retired from office.

Thomas Jefferson abandoned religion after learning about the new age's revolutionary philosophy, and this enclosed his liberal ideas. He was an avid reader of John Locke, so he knew how to justify the English colonies' rebellions during the late 1700s.

Fact: Despite his independence ideals, he had more than 600 slaves in his power, justifying these facts with racist arguments. Practically the United States that he dreamed of was one without "the black race."

An amazing fact was that he loved to hear mockingbirds sing and hence kept them as pets.

JAMES MADISON

1809-1817

 Virginia

Democrat-Republican

He is considered the 'father of the Constitution' and one of the men who made the United States an independent nation. Despite his ideals of freedom and justice, he was also a slave owner.

A rumor has spread over the years that Madison was a Freemason. However, there is no official evidence to verify this information. During his tenure, the debt that the emerging independent country had acquired decreased, and taxes were also lowered.

Fact: He was one of the shortest presidents in the United States, as he was only 1.63 meters tall.

He was Hebrew among other subjects at Princeton University's and was their very first graduate student.

JAMES MONROE

1817-1825

Virginia

Democrat-Republican

The fifth president of the United States followed the line of the Democrats-Republicans, serving as Secretary of State before coming to power, and belonged to the 'Virginia Dynasty'. He faced an economic crisis that caused high unemployment in the country and approved the purchase of Florida from Spain in 1819.

Fact: One of the most remembered actions of this president without a doubt, is the Monroe Doctrine ("America for Americans"), which imposes severe limits on European intervention in the Western Hemisphere.

He was also a law apprentice for Thomas Jefferson before delving into politics.

JOHN QUINCY ADAMS

1825-1829

Massachusetts

Republican Democrat

Adams had experience as a lawyer and senator before assuming the presidency. Throughout his political career, he paraded for a large number of parties. His father, John Adams, is still considered one of the United States' founding fathers today.

As a leader in the Massachusetts House of Representatives, he was considered an abolitionist and believed that slavery could be canceled if the country faced a warlike conflict.

Fact: His death took place in the Washington Capitol, and it is believed that his last words were: "This is the end of the Earth, I am happy."

He skinny-dipped every morning at the Potomac River.

ANDREW JACKSON

1829-1837

North Carolina

Democrat

The family of this president came from the migrations of Ireland and Scotland. When he was only thirteen years old, he was captured by the English, who tortured and ill-treated him by making him a prisoner of war.

In power, he faced secession from South Carolina and supported Martin Van Buren's campaign for the presidency as his successor. He decentralized the economy, took on wealthy bankers, and went down in history with the creation of Jacksonian democracy.

Fact: He was the only president of the United States to be a prisoner of war, and his foreign policy was taken over by presidents like Donald Trump.

This president had a gigantic block of cheese weighing 1,400 pounds which he kept in the White House, and only after he left the presidency did he let the public eat a block of cheddar.

MARTIN VAN BUREN

1837-1842

New York

Democrat

During Martin Van Buren's tenure, he consolidated the Democratic Party and faced an economic crisis that destabilized all social sectors. This caused Van Buren to become a president not well accepted by the people and had difficulties being re-elected.

Fact: The issue of slavery caused and the economic crisis made the Van Buren government lose popularity among voters.

Another sad fact was that president Buren lost his wife in 1819, and never remarried. The first lady duties were filled in by his daughter-in-law.

WILLIAM HENRY HARRISON

1841 to 1841

Virginia

Whig

Harrison's passage through U.S. politics was brief, as the president barely spent a month in power before his sudden death, which once again destabilized the credibility of American democracy.

Harrison was an important war hero who the people of the United States loved. His career as Secretary of the Northwest Territory is one aspect of his career that transcended history, and today, he is remembered for his outstanding military strategies.

Fact: He was the oldest president to assume power until Ronald Reagan's victory. He died after spending only 32 days in office after his one hour, 45 minutes' inauguration speech a month before in a snowstorm which is the longest to date.

JOHN TYLER

1841 to 1845

Virginia

Whig/Independent

Harrison's successor opposed his veto on the creation of the National Bank and carried out the agreement to annex Texas to the American Union. He sought to serve as president before Congress with the same prerogatives as Harrison, and consequently, he obtained the support of both houses. He created the country's Center for Meteorological Studies and ended the war against the Seminole Indians of Florida.

Fact: Basically, this president is remembered for extending U.S. territory in the southern zone with Texas's accession. He also had 15 children.

JAMES KNOX POLK

1845-1849

North Carolina

Democrat

James K. Polk continued the legacy of Tyler. He ended up signing the annexation of Texas to the United States. Due to these events, an important war took place between Spain and the United States, which took place in the states of Arizona, New Mexico, California, and Nevada.

It is because of him that the U.S. border moved towards the Rio Grande and the Pacific Ocean.

Fact: During his government, Polk integrated new territories into the American union and proposed to Spain the purchase of Cuba for 100 million dollars.

He also oversaw the issuing of the first postage stamp and presided over the Washington Monument building.

ZACHARY TAYLOR

1849-1850

Virginia

Whig

Another U.S. president who stood out for his military strategies was, without a doubt, Zachary Taylor, who developed a great struggle against the native peoples of North America and had strong tensions with Mexico over the annexation of territories.

His presidency was practically appointed by Polk, with whom he had made a great alliance in the search to take over Texas and the rest of the territories belonging to Mexico.

Fact: Zachary's pragmatic coldness is something difficult to forget, as it led him to star in turbulent episodes such as the murder of hundreds of civilians in the Spanish territory.

MILLARD FILLMORE

1850 to 1853

New York

Whig

Fillmore, despite being president, never won the election, taking office after Taylor's death.

He belonged to two political parties, the Anti-Masonic and the Whig, with which he became the White House president. He was a candidate for the American / Nativist Party and has sadly been remembered for mediocre rather than historical turnout.

Fact: Despite his modest historical legacy, this president had a surprising political career that began at the age of 24, in the military with the Anti-Masonic Party. He also didn't have a vice president during his time in the presidency.

FRANKLIN PIERCE

1853-1857

New Hampshire

Democrat

For Franklin Pierce, the abolitionist movement posed a threat to the nation and its prosperity. With the signing of the Kansas-Nebraska Law, he managed to distance himself from the antislavery groups and thus sought to stop the strong tensions between the North and the South of the United States.

He created profitable commercial alliances with Great Britain and Japan while his cabinet devised their departments' reform. However, he was severely criticized for the Ostend Manifesto, which called for the annexation of Cuba.

Fact: Pierce's reputation declined as his criticism of Lincoln increased.

JAMES BUCHANAN

1857-1863

Pennsylvania

Democrat

Buchanan has been harshly criticized over the years for maintaining a lukewarm stance in the face of the division of the country with the outbreak of the Civil War, however, he maintained a great work in progress throughout the years prior to his tenure.

Fact: Buchanan is the first president to come from Pennsylvania and the most severely criticized by historians and specialists.

Buchanan was a completely unmarried person till he left office.

ABRAHAM LINCOLN

1861-1865

Kentucky

Republican National Union

This American politician and lawyer is one of the most important presidents of the United States. He was the one who led the nation against the Civil War and preserved as far as possible stability in the American union.

After he won the elections, the south of the country rose up and declared that secession was inevitable. At this time, the assassination attempts against the president began with one in Baltimore, which made Lincoln have to arrive in Washington secretly.

Fact: Lincoln has been considered the president who abolished slavery in the United States, but with certain limitations.

He is presently in the Wrestling Hall of Fame because he only lost one match out of the 300 matches he participated in as a young wrestler.

ANDREW JOHNSON

1865-1869

North Carolina

Democratic National Union/Independent National Union

After Lincoln's assassination, Andrew Johnson came to power with the backing of Democrats with the Civil War unfolding as the background. This led him to seek to rebuild relations with those states that had separated from the American Union. However, the apparent wounds were deep and manifested with the opposition of the Republican majority in Congress.

Fact: Johnson was the first president to be impeached and the first to try to unify the country after the Civil War.

He also never attended school and taught himself how to read.

ULYSSES S. GRANT

1869-1877

Ohio

Republican

Grant first held the position of commanding general of the United States Army. He worked closely with Lincoln and led important armies to victory.

On the economic side, he promoted a time of prosperity. During his eight years, he was also subject to strong criticism by his opponents. The economic depression of 1873 was the most complicated of his government.

Fact: Grant wanted to expand the U.S. territory and looked for a way to annex the Dominican Republic without great success.

The "S" initial in his name actually means nothing; it was a result of a clerical error.

RUTHERFORD B. HAYES

1877-1881

Ohio

Republican

Rutherford continued with the national reconstruction initiated by his predecessors.

His government's great success was the recovery of confidence in politics by the Americans, which earned Hayes to be considered a reformist in aspects of public function.

From the beginning of his mandate, he promised that he would not seek re-election, and once his first term in power was over, he kept his promise.

Fact: Historical rumors have that Hayes was the first president to know about Graham Bell's invention: the telephone.

He was the first president to be sworn in privately on Saturday in the White House. Rutherford later swore the oath in public.

JAMES A. GARFIELD

1881-1881,

Ohio

Republican

This president starred in the second shortest term in the history of the American union. He was a candidate for the Republican Party and took advantage of the rivalry that existed between his opponents to gain popularity.

It is believed that party members chose him for being a little-known candidate with a manipulable reputation; however, once in power, he faced a complicated enmity with the Stalwarts.

Fact: At 26, he became the president of Eclectic Institute, his college.

Also, After Lincoln, he was the second president to be assassinated.

CHESTER A. ARTHUR

1881 to 1885

Vermont

Republican

Chester A. Arthur served as president after Garfield's death. He was sworn in on two counts and believed that by maintaining an independent stance on clientelism and the civil service system, he could successfully navigate these complicated separations.

He determined to apply his own ways in the White House and relieved all members of Garfield's cabinet.

Fact: He tried to reduce tariffs on foreign policy and enacted the first general Federal Law on immigration.

GROVER CLEVELAND

1885-1889

New Jersey

Democrat

Cleveland did not have consecutive terms but was the only Democrat to reach the presidency in a difficult time for this side.

He was extremely popular among the population and critics, although the latter highlights that the second term was in contrast to the first because he faced a serious economic crisis in which he lost control of his party.

Fact: Cleveland's idea was to achieve an effective and transparent government that would benefit its nation. He followed classical liberalism and is credited with the phrase, "I only have one thing to do, and that is to do the right thing."

BENJAMIN HARRISON

1889-1893

Ohio

Republican

Politics surrounded Benjamin from an early age. The blood of the first independence revolutionaries ran in his family, and this echoed his ideals.

Despite being a man with a cold and reserved character, his demand made sense when contrasted with the great goals he had for his nation during his government. His pragmatism earned him strong criticism from his opponents, such as Theodore Roosevelt.

With him, Republicans won a strong majority in the Senate and the House of Representatives.

Fact: Like his personality, the story recalls Harrison in the midst of a hermetic process that included severe economic and public policy reforms. He was the first president to enjoy electricity in the White House. Although for fear of electric shock, he and his wife refused to touch the lights.

WILLIAM MCKINLEY

1897 to 1901

Republican

Ohio

Although after Benjamin Harrison it was Cleveland who assumed power, he was preceded by William McKinley of the Republican flock, occupying the 25th position in the presidency of the United States.

The republican domain began from his stay in power and encouraged commercial activity. He was elected president again in 1900 and supported the independence of Cuba.

Fact: During his campaign, the use of new advertising techniques like telephone campaigning that would forever change the dissemination of political messages in the United States stood out.

THEODORE ROOSEVELT

1901 to 1909

New York

Republican

One of the most popular presidents of the United States, without a doubt, is Theodore Roosevelt, who with his exuberant, outgoing personality and innate leadership, managed to be remembered for his social activism, the reform of his country, and his time at the forefront of the Progressive Movement.

Fact: Roosevelt is one of the few American presidents who publicly announced the fight against corruption in the political spheres of the country. He also watched the funeral procession of Lincoln when he was a child.

WILLIAM HOWARD TAFT

1909-1913

Ohio

Republican

Although William Howard was successful in his administration, the firing of Gifford Pinchot as Chief of the United States Forest Service fragmented his relationship with Roosevelt and seriously affected the Republican Party.

Throughout his tenure, he enacted a series of policies that affected tariffs and transportation rates.

Fact: he was the only U.S. president to attain the position simultaneously as he was president of the Supreme Court.

WOODROW WILSON

1913-1921

Virginia

Democrat

Woodrow was in charge of bringing the Progressive Movement to the White House and promising that the United States would maintain a neutral position before the outbreak of the First World War. However, at the same time that his government began, the Revolution broke out in Mexico, which further complicated things in the border area of both nations.

Fact: In contrast to his protectionist and nationalist policies, Wilson prevented women and African Americans from having full rights.

He nominated the first Jewish justice to the Supreme Court.

WARREN G. HARDING

1921-1923

Ohio

Republican

During his administration, Harding advocated for labor reform and created the foundation for implementing the eight-hour day. It secured the annulment of the Anglo-Japanese Alliance and provided federal grants for state programs focused on health care for mothers and children.

Fact: He has been considered a "lukewarm" president since he did not achieve one of his mandate's main goals: to stabilize peaceful economic development in the Far East.

CALVIN COOLIDGE

1923-1929

Vermont

Republican

Coolidge inherited the economic, political, and social problems that Harding accumulated throughout his government. He based his success on a campaign to keep calm in "difficult" times and advocated for a more economical and efficient government in which the goal was to reduce federal taxes as well as the national debt.

Fact: Vetoed the Bonus Bill, thereby blocking additional payments for WWI veterans.

HERBERT HOOVER

1929-1933

Iowa

Republican

When Herbert came to power, he was applauded for his progressive platform and extensive knowledge of economics, for which it was believed that he had very good judgment for these exercises.

As the nation's supreme leader, Hoover had to manage the country in the midst of one of the most significant economic and political crises in history: the stock market crash and the Great Depression of 1929.

Fact: Hoover was a graduate of geology from Stanford University and a self-made millionaire.

The Hoover government was marked by the Great Depression, one of the most catastrophic economic crises that this country has faced throughout its history.

FRANKLIN DELANO ROOSEVELT

1933-1945

New York

Democrat

Thanks to Delano, the Democratic caucus was able to secure a position within the White House. Because in the face of the economic crisis, urgent measures were needed.

His political campaign consisted of letting Hoover drown alone, and thus, with his growing unpopularity, Delano came to office without complications.

Fact: He was practically the savior of the American economy after the great blow of the Great Depression.

He also collected stamps as a hobby and stress reliever in the White House.

HARRY S. TRUMAN

1945-1953

Missouri

Democrat

During his tenure, the beginning of the Cold War was created, and for this reason, Truman committed his country to the containment of Soviet expansionism.

At the end of his career, his return to politics was one of the most impressive in American history, winning the presidency in his own right.

Fact: During his tenure, the North Atlantic Treaty Organization (NATO) was created and ratified in 1949.

DWIGHT D. EISENHOWER

1953-1961

Texas

Republican

During the Cold War, Eisenhower sought an active containment campaign that worked alongside his proposal for "an early and honorable peace." During his government, the space race began with the launch of Soviet Sputnik, which encouraged the United States to apply a series of programs that will improve the nation in every way.

Fact: Dwight orchestrated the creation of functional infrastructure and mobilized federal troops to Arkansas to protect African American students after the desegregation of Central High School was abolished and was actively involved in defending South Vietnam.

He also named Camp David after his grandson, David.

JOHN F. KENNEDY

1961-1963

Massachusetts

Democrat

Kennedy, the thirty-fifth president of the United States.

His proposal against conservatism earned him harsh criticism from this side, and the arms race against the USSR was one of the greatest challenges for his government. His murder and the motives behind it remain a mystery, yet his legacy is a source of inspiration for promising youngsters to become present in the United States.

Fact: during his government, man reached the moon, but he also started one of the saddest periods of the Cold War with the Berlin Wall's lifting.

Kennedy also donated his entire White House salary to charity.

LYNDON B. JOHNSON

1963-1969

Texas

Democrat

After the Kennedy assassination, Lyndon B. Johnson was the person elected to the presidency. In his election campaign, he declared a "war on poverty" and challenged Americans to build a great society together.

Fact: Although Lyndon's intentions to enhance life and dignity in the United States' interior were a success in his plan of activities; the Vietnam War ended up condemning his mandate.

RICHARD NIXON

1969-1974

California

Republican

Nixon bet the support of his candidacy to the most conservative part of the United States. However, in the whole world, revolutions were brewing that sought to transform the forms of thought to move them away from obsolete conservatism.

Fact: Nixon resigned after starring in a scandal known as Watergate, and with this, he became the first and only president to resign from his position in the United States.

GERALD FORD

1974 to 1977

Nebraska

Republican

After Nixon's resignation, Gerald Ford came to power and tried to tackle a series of actions that would bring economic stability to the nation, but he was unsuccessful in these attempts.

In addition to this, his administration faced an energy crisis and had to refocus the population's attention on Watergate.

Fact: in 1975, issued the emergency evacuation for the soldiers remaining in Vietnam.

Ford was the only politician known to serve as both vice president and president without actually being elected.

JIMMY CARTER

1977-1981

Georgia

Democrat

After the Vietnam War, confidence in the American government was undermined. Therefore, the emergence of Jimmy Carter as a political candidate made people look at him less suspiciously.

Carter faced a weak economy and rising inflation. The war problems with Iran earned him several episodes where terrorism took over, and his mandate ended up being condemned.

Fact: He received the Nobel Peace Prize and partly recovered the trust that the Nixon government broke. Carter also created the Department of Energy due to the energy shortage problem.

RONALD REAGAN

1981-1989

Illinois

Republican

For the United States, Ronald Reagan epitomized "the recovery of conservatism," and his transition from conservative activism to the pursuit of the presidency has been criticized for the media influence that his political career gained.

Fact: During his tenure, there was a strong passivity in the face of the AIDS crisis that affected dozens of people.

According to his wife, Reagan was a fussy eater.

GEORGE H.W BUSH

1989 to 1993

Massachusetts

Republican

George Bush Sr. affirmed that he would not raise taxes throughout his term and ran a

campaign in which he promised to preserve the works of previous administrations. He tried to balance the budget and stabilized the economy but was severely criticized for his inability to accomplish this task.

Fact: The Bush Senior administration is remembered more for the "positive" changes it had with foreign affairs than domestic policy.

In the Navy, he was the youngest pilot when he served.

BILL CLINTON

1993-2001

Arkansas

Democrat

Clinton was the third-youngest president in the U.S. nation and defeated George HW Bush in the 1992 elections. He served two terms, and throughout history, his image was taken up in different aspects of popular culture.

Fact: He established good relations with political figures such as Tony Blair, Jacques Chirac, Carlos Salinas de Gortari, Fernando Henrique Cardoso, and Rafael Caldera, among others.

He has also won two Grammys. First for the album "Prokofiev" and the second, his autobiography, "My Life."

GEORGE W. BUSH

2001 to 2009

Connecticut

Republican

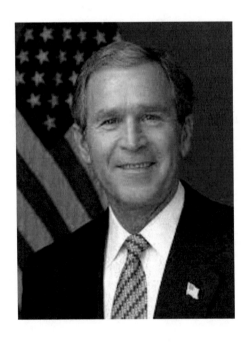

George W. Bush was another American president with a long line of political backgrounds in his family. His father held power, and when the Republican ascended to the government, many were the speculations generated by it.

In his government, same-sex marriage was banned, economic, health, and social security policies were promoted, as well as abortion issues.

Fact: He was a co-owner of the Texas Rangers baseball team, and within eight months of starting his term, he faced one of the most memorable terrorist attacks in the United States: the attack on the Twin Towers.

Bush graduated from Harvard Business School in 1975 and was the first president with an MBA.

BARACK OBAMA

2009 to 2017

Hawaii

Democrat

Barack Obama went down in history as a president who changed some of America's most important paradigms.

During his tenure, he passed a series of reforms to solve the economic problems accumulated during 2008, showed the efficiency of the U.S. military and security strategies with the capture and elimination of Osama bin Laden and developed social programs to support health such as Obamacare and the Dhaka.

Fact: in addition to being the first president of African-American origin to take office in the United States, he won an ironic Nobel Peace Prize, and his government reached the highest number of deported Mexicans.

His first job was selling ice cream at Baskin Robbins. He no longer likes ice cream because he ate so much of it.

DONALD TRUMP

2017 to 2020

New York

Republican

Donald Trump came to power in 2017 after a controversial campaign that won him victory against Democrat Hilary Clinton.

Fact: He is one of the most controversial presidents in recent United States history, the second to face impeachment, and one of the most controversial for his classist ideas and polarizing opinions. He lost the 2020 election to his opponent on the Democratic side, Joe Biden.

Donald Trump has also appeared in some movies, including "Home Alone 2." and "Zoolander".

JOE BIDEN

2021-

Pennsylvania

Democrat

Joe Biden is present president of the United States, and his term will span from 2020 to 2024. After a controversial contest against Donald Trump, he achieved virtual victory after being elected in the state of Pennsylvania.

Some of the essential points of his campaign are the promotion of the use of clean energy, greater access to education and health, and the objective of rebuilding the relationships and alliances that the United States had prior to the arrival of Donald Trump to the presidency.

Fact: He is the presidential candidate with the most votes in the history of the United States. Also, at 30 years of age, he was elected as a senator for the first time. He held this position from 1973 to 2008. He was instrumental in achieving reforms such as Obamacare and the withdrawal of troops from the Middle East. Biden is the oldest president in the history of the U.S. at age 78.

QUIZ

1) What is the name of the first U.S president to get impeached?

_____

_____

_____

_____

_____

_____

_____

2) Why was Warren G. Harding considered a lukewarm?

_____

_____

_____

_____

_____

_____

3) During whose tenure did the attack on the Twins tower occur?

_____

_____

_____

_____

_____

_____

_____

4) What is the reason why Nixon resigned?

_____

_____

_____

_____

_____

_____

_____

5) Who was the first president to know about the telephone?

_____

_____

_____

_____

_____

_____

_____

6) Name 2 U.S presidents who were assassinated

_____

_____

_____

_____

_____

_____

7) "I only have one thing to do, and that is to do the right thing." Who said that?

_____

_____

_____

_____

_____

_____

_____

8) Who was the president when Mexicans were largely deported?

_____

_____

_____

_____

_____

_____

_____

9) James Madison was a slave owner 'Yes' or 'No'?

_____

_____

_____

_____

_____

_____

10)   **Who proposed selling Cuba to Spain?**

_____

_____

_____

_____

_____

_____

_____

BONUS PAGES

GUESS AND COLOR

WHO IS THIS? _____

GUESS AND COLOR

WHO IS THIS? _____

Made in the USA
Thornton, CO
04/26/24 14:13:31

111fde07-f576-4151-a8e9-8fe3cf3738acR01